BECOME A REAL
BUDDHIST

Other publications by Brian F. Taylor

BLONDIN Collected Poems
BAMBOO LEAVES Poetry in Thailand
OXFORD BLUES Poetry in Oxford
CENTRE The Truth about Everything
BASIC BUDDHISM FOR A WORLD IN TROUBLE
BASIC BUDDHISM SERIES (Ten booklets)
FOR HUMANITY MEMORY HAS COME TO
REPLACE UNDERSTANDING

BECOME A REAL BUDDHIST

from Talks by

Brian Taylor

Edited by
Linden Brough

道

Universal Octopus Publication

Talks collected in 2009

🛡

COPYRIGHT © 2011 *Ariya*
First Edition 2011. Second Edition 2025

ISBN 978-1-8384024-2-6

A catalogue record of this book is available from the
British Library.

Published by Universal Octopus 2025
www.universaloctopus.com

"Owners of their karma are beings, heirs of their karma,
their karma is the womb from which they are born,
their karma is their friend, their refuge. Whatever karma they
perform, good or bad, thereof they will be the heirs."

(Majjhima Nikaya, 135)

"Volition, O Bhikkhus, is what I call karma; for through
volition, one performs actions of body, speech and mind."

(Anguttara Nikaya 6: 63)

CONTENTS

PART 1

THE FIVE BUDDHIST PRECEPTS

"I undertake to observe the precept to abstain from killing living beings.

I undertake to observe the precept to abstain from taking things not given.

I undertake to observe the precept to abstain from sexual misconduct.

I undertake to observe the precept to abstain from false speech.

I undertake to observe the precept to abstain from intoxicating drinks and drugs causing heedlessness."

INTRODUCTION

W hat do you think will happen to you if you were to *die* tonight?

"I don't really know but have a sense of being born in a higher realm. Sometimes it is so miserable here in this world that I'm ready to die knowing it will be better. I keep the Five Precepts and strive earnestly with the practice of Dāna, Sīla and Bhāvanā."

That's all very well but you are still trapped in the Sangsāra. You go *up* when there is enough merit and when that runs out, *down* you fall. Continuously. Including all the way down to the Hell realms. There is so much karma from the past still to ripen – waiting to drag one down. Some of us have some very bad karma from the past still to be accounted for.

"If one becomes a Stream-enterer, a Sotāpanna, wouldn't that save one from ever again falling down to the Hell worlds?"

That is true. Becoming a Sotāpanna, a Stream-enterer, locks *forever* the gates to the Peta, Animal and Hell realms. How would you know that you were a Stream-enterer?

"The Dhamma books say that it is by getting rid of the First Three Fetters - Belief in a Self, Sceptical Doubt and Attachment to Rule and Ritual. I have complete faith in the Buddha's Teaching, very little sign of attachment to Rite and Ritual and belief in a Self is diminishing..."

You have given three answers and scored nothing out of three. Do you know the story of Gulliver?

"Yes."

There he is lying on the ground all tied up and unable to move. Now, if you can imagine that he is tied up by *ten* ropes representing the Ten Fetters, if he had managed to undo or get rid of *three*, he might be able to sit up and work at liberating himself from the others. He would *know* that he had begun to free himself and have some enthusiasm and energy to continue.

It's very difficult to come across perfect translations from the Pali of exactly what the Buddha taught. Much of what we have to work with is from translations from people like Miss Horner and Rhys Davids, who had not attained themselves the states they were translating into English.

Let's look up what Nyānatiloka says about the *'First Three Fetters'* in his Buddhist Dictionary. It should be fairly close to the real thing because of his background and attainment.

The Pali for 'Fetters' is 'samyojana' and it says:

> **samyojana:**
> There are Ten Fetters tying beings down to the Wheel of Existence. He who is free of the first three is a Sotāpanna, or Stream-Winner i.e. one who has entered the stream to Nibbāna...
>
> The First Three Fetters are:-
>
> *1.* Personalty Belief *(sakkāya-diṭṭhi)*
> *2.* What is called "Sceptical Doubt" *(vicikicchā)*

3. What is called "Clinging to mere Rules and Ritual" *(sīlabbata-parāmāsa)*

This word 'personality' keeps cropping up in the various Dhamma books. What does it mean? Can you be sure *"I have got rid of personality belief"*? Let's look at the Pali, 'sakkāya-diṭṭhi', they are translating from:-

sakkāya-diṭṭhi:
Personality belief, is the first of the Ten Fetters *(Samyojana)*. It is entirely abandoned only on reaching the Path of Stream-Winning *(Sotāpatti magga)*. There are 20 kinds of 'Personality Belief' which are obtained by applying 4 types of that belief to each of the 5 Khandhas *(Corporeality, Feeling, Perception, Mental Formations and Consciousness)*.

Now, this is getting closer... Let's take the 4 types of belief and apply them to 'corporeality', or 'body', the first Khandha:-

4 Types of Belief:
To be *identified* with 'the body'
To be *contained* in 'the body'
To be *independent* of 'the body'
To be *owner* of 'the body'

This is the real meaning of the First Fetter – getting rid of attachment to *'the body'* as anything to do with oneself. Thus 'sakkāya-diṭṭhi' means 'Own Body Views'. This is the First Fetter to be removed.

The Second Fetter, 'Sceptical Doubt' *(vicikicchā)*, is not got rid of by mere *faith* alone. Let's look it up:-

vicikicchā:
Sceptical doubt, one of the five Hindrances and one of the
first three Fetters, which disappear forever at Stream-
entry.
As a Fetter, it refers to sceptical doubt about the Buddha,
the Dhamma, and the Sangha (the Teacher, the Teaching,
and the Training); doubt about things past and future, and
conditionality. It also applies to uncertainty about whether
things are wholesome or not, to be practised or not, of high
or low value etc.

According to Visuddhimagga, 'Path of Purification', it is a
lack of desire to think; it has the nature of *wavering* and its
manifestation is *indecision* and a *divided attitude*: its
proximate cause is unwise attention to matters of doubt.

The Buddha didn't teach us to have *faith* in his teaching
like the faith-practice of other religions. He taught it as a
Dhamma which is *self-realised*, a *come-and-see* thing – to
test it out for yourselves.

What it means is that having put the Dhamma into
practice, one would *experience for oneself* the result. Faith
would not then come into it because having tested a little
successfully there would be confidence that the rest of the
Teaching is also true.

This confidence is based on investigation *not* belief. This
is what the Second Fetter is referring to – *knowing* and
seeing for oneself. Thus 'vicikicchā' means 'Doubt'.

The Third Fetter is *'sīlabbata-parāmāsa'*. Let's look this
one up:-

sīlabbata-parāmāsa:
Clinging to mere rules and ritual... The holding firmly

to the view that through mere rules and ritual one may reach purification.

'Sīla' gives the clue. This Fetter refers to one's *sīla,* one's morality. In the texts a Sotāpanna is referred to as having *perfect morality.* They keep perfectly the Five Precepts. A Sotāpanna cannot break one.

This Fetter has nothing to do with rituals of lighting candles, incense, bowing, bathing in the Ganges etc.; it is strictly related to morality. It is *clinging* to real morality which creates the fetter, deriving satisfaction from your behaviour, allowing an opinion of yourself to arise (see First Fetter) such as "I am one who practises morality". Thus 'sīlabbata-parāmāsa' means 'Clinging to Morality'. This has to be got rid of.

The attainment of Stream-entry *(Sotāpanna)* is what one would wish for everyone, particularly one's family and friends – *the safety of a Stream-enterer.* Knowing this, one can let them go, knowing they will *always* be safe. (However, there are very, very few who attain this state...)

The First Three Fetters are:-

1. Own Body Views *(sakkāya-diṭṭhi)*
2. Doubt *(vicikicchā)*
3. Clinging to Morality *(sīlabbata-parāmāsa)*

Now it can be clear *if* one has attained Stream-entry, and, if not, just what needs to be done.

REMOVING THE FIRST
THREE FETTERS

A good man has good thoughts and he is happy. He will try and make the world a better place. When he dies, he will go to heaven for a little while and then come back again.

A practising Buddhist would have good thoughts, be a good man and be happy. He will not be working to make the world a better place; he will be practising to escape the world.

Many have viewed the world as a prison camp and tried to escape from it. They dig tunnels etc. only to reappear somewhere else in the prison camp.

Everything has to be let go.

Very few understand this – both the pleasant and the unpleasant have to be *let go* to escape. The way to escape is to make it your *goal* and adjust your life in such a way as to be able to practise *continuously*. The Buddha, after seeing to his basic needs and giving Dhamma Talks, would meditate. Do what needs to be done then meditate.

The actual practice is the Noble Eightfold Path.

It's quite simple but difficult to do because the mind is used to being *stirred up*. One needs to watch out for thoughts that stir the mind up – actions, and particularly speech, all create karma, and *more* stirring up.

WATCH the mind continuously – *mind comes first*.

STOP following trains of thought.

NIP thought patterns at the acorn stage before too much energy is generated – and you get lost! If you were to die at that stage, you would have no idea where you might be reborn. As the mind would be in an unwholesome state – an unwholesome rebirth might follow.

STRIVE for the development of Samatha and Vipassana.

This is what is needed to be done to *escape* from the prison camp – escape from the world. (But perhaps you don't really want to but are quite content to enjoy the pleasant? Be truthful to yourself either way – at least know what you really want.)

- The practice is in letting go and this will accelerate as the *sense contact* is noted sooner.

- First there is the letting go of what has been *grasped.*

- Then there is the letting go of *reaching out* which is without any pain at all and very rapid.

- Then there is letting go of even the *slightest reaching out.*

Keep this practice up to remove the First Three Fetters.

FIRST THREE-LEGGED STOOL

S o, what if you manage to achieve a comfortable life: Body, Mind and Daily Work? To have a comfortable balance that's not too problematic? You can sit on the 'First Three-Legged Stool' comfortably – what for?

Eventually you will fall off and *die!* Life is a disintegrating process, each breath taking *you* nearer to your *last* breath. Each day passing is one *less* day of life left. What's it all about?

When you die, you lose *everything* – body, possessions, home, family, friends...

What's the best thing to do with a comfortable life?

IT IS ESSENTIAL TO TAKE CONTROL

Tick, Tick, Tick, Tick... The mind is ticking away all the time.

Tick, Tick, Tick, Tick... The days are passing away all the time.

Tick, Tick, Tick, Tick... It's as though one is walking *all* the time... Morning, afternoon, evening, going to sleep, dreaming, waking, morning again... And this goes on, and on, and on - birth to death, over and over again.

It is experienced as Suffering.

One could be walking East or West, South or North, it could be Dhamma walking, or Mammon walking, or Mindful walking... Without taking control of *where* the 'walk' is going – karma takes over and one goes *up* with good karma and *down* with bad karma.

It is essential to take control of the direction one is walking – and *not* be driven by karma.

PERSEVERANCE IS NEEDED

M ore perseverance is required when understanding is weak.

The more understanding, the less perseverance is required. For example, 95% perseverance is needed for 5% understanding. 50% perseverance is needed for 50% understanding. 30% perseverance for 70% understanding and so on...

One must not let up on *perseverance*.

UNDERSTANDING
CONDITIONED GENESIS

Visākha Pujā (the full moon day in May on which the Buddha was Born, became Enlightened, and Passed Away) is a special Uposatha Day. It is a public holiday in Buddhist countries. A lot of merit is made. It is the equivalent to Easter in the Christian calendar – Easter being the showing, the demonstration, that *body is not self* with Christ's Resurrection.

What the Buddha discovered was a remarkable achievement. Most Buddhists have difficulty in understanding Conditioned Genesis which is what the Buddha worked out on the night of his Enlightenment.

He had fully attained the Eight Jhānas but still knew that he hadn't reached Enlightenment. So, he worked with the *actual reality* of what was being presented at the sense doors. And this is what he found: -

IGNORANCE
conditions
SANKHĀRAS
which condition
CONSCIOUSNESS
which condition
NĀMA RŪPA
which condition
SIX SENSE BASES
which condition
CONTACT
which condition
FEELING
which condition

CRAVING
which condition
CLINGING
which condition
BECOMING
which condition
BIRTH
which condition
DEATH, SICKNESS, OLD AGE…

The phenomena that the Buddha studied with *direct experience* were the Sankhāras. He then saw that the *whole of the* sangsāra was kept going by them.

Once he had deduced all this, and gone through it several times, he found his mind to be completely enlightened. He understood the whole process of existence and the Four Noble Truths: -

The Noble Truth of Suffering (*dukkha*).

The Noble Truth of the Origin of Suffering (*dukkha–samudaya*).

The Noble Truth of the Extinction of Suffering (*dukkha– nirodha*).

The Noble Truth of the Path that leads to the Extinction of Suffering (*dukkha–nirodha–gāmini–paṭipadā).*

WHAT ARE SANKHĀRAS?

S ankhāras are things which are held together by conditions and fall apart because of conditions. Everything in the universe is a sankhāra.

When the body is viewed in this way, there is *no* self, *no* 'atta', to be found. When everything is investigated in this light – everything is seen as impermanent, therefore without self, and unsatisfacory.

The Mind that clearly sees this in *all* phenomena changes! It is a spontaneous change as a result of clear seeing for oneself. It is a practical result *not* to be obtained from reading or study.

The sankhāras are *real*.

Suffering is *real*.

SEEING the three characteristics (*aniccā, dukkha* and *anattā)*, is *not* enough. It is penetration of the *Four Noble Truths* and a practical understanding from personal discovery of *Dependent Origination.*

ALL FORMATIONS ARE SANKHĀRAS

I t is right that all formations are sankhāras.

We don't need to complicate it by separating or grouping them. We are investigating to understand sankhāra itself, though it is true that there is *rūpa-sankhāra* and *nāma-sankhāra* but the sankhāras are the same in nature.

"I tried to find a model of sankhāra for you and started at the Early Learning Centre. I found one in the age range of 12 months to 3 years... There is one for each of you – please build your sankhāras..."

(We were each given a brown envelope containing a small wooden jigsaw of 6 pieces. Everyone had an Animal with its young – a Cow and Calf, a Sheep and Lamb, a Duck and Duckling and so on...)

Now, what is putting the sankhāras together is karmic effort! What you have built you give a name but look, as time passes... it breaks up... it ages... loses bits and eventually falls apart (and here this was demonstrated by the pieces of the jigsaw being separated...) until there is nothing left as the bits separate into dissolution. There is nothing left to reincarnate. There is *no self.* It is *impermanent* and therefore *unsatisfactory.*

That's all there is to know about a sankhāra. Yet there have been long definitions and books written on the subject. It is this simple, but this *seeing* has the effect of *understanding* that everything in the universe is unsatisfactory.

Nibbāna has no sankhāras and therefore is completely free from *suffering*, free from *unsatisfactoriness,* and it is free from *a self.* It isn't annihilation.

If you understand this, this far, and continue with practice, in time – dependent on *karma* and *merit* – you will reach Nibbāna for certain.

SPONTANEOUS CHANGE OF VIEW

W hen one sees a bit of an animal on one's plate, that *seeing* of the *actual reality*, causes a spontaneous change! A stopping of eating meat that can never be reversed.

It is the same with sankhāras.

When knowledge arises from one's *own* direct experience of them, there is a spontaneous change of view.

One recoils from them, is disgusted by them, turns away from them towards deliverance from them, towards a state *free* from sankhāras, to Nibbāna.

There is *no* need now for restraint or further striving and perseverance when this occurs. It is a natural process based on right understanding of the phenomena at the *sense doors* – continuously (twenty-four hours a day – seven days a week).

THE SECOND THREE-LEGGED STOOL

T he three legs of the 'Second Three-Legged Stool'
are:-

- *SAMĀDHI* – One Pointedness

- *PAÑÑĀ* – Right Understanding

- *SATI* – Mindfulness

'Sati' has always been translated as Mindfulness, which is
a rather difficult definition when the aim is to have an
empty mind. Remembrance or Recollection might be a
more helpful definition when one is practising *letting go*
of all phenomena that are arising at the six sense doors.

To let go of something, it first has to be recognized and
labelled correctly. Otherwise, it flows into a stream of
thought, feeling, perception etc. and one has *missed*
letting go.

Recognise phenomena in whatever category one is
working with. If a thought can be recognised as just a
thought and let go – that's fine.

If one is working with the *Three Characteristics*, then
using them to recognise *impermanence, unsatisfactoriness*
and *non-self* would enable letting go.

Or if recognising the various *Sense Consciousnesses* –
that works too.

Or the *Hindrances...* Or the *Five Khandhas...* Or the
Factors of Enlightenment...

The important thing is to recognise the phenomenon *as it arises* through one of the Four Foundations of Mindfulness; *Body, Feeling, Citta* and *Dhamma* - otherwise it *cannot* be let go.

When the 'three legs' come into balance: -

- One Pointedness (*samādhi*)
- Right Understanding *(paññā)*
- Mindfulness *(sati)*

and are working perfectly; they disappear. What replaces them is *experience.* This is what one is aiming for.

GOING OUT THERE IS NO OTHER, COMING BACK THERE IS NO TRACE

We were each given a symbol drawn on a blank postcard. One side was a drawing of what was called the 'Universal Octopus' and the other side had an empty circle which was called 'The Source'.

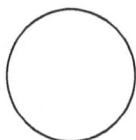

We were asked to draw a *dotted line* at the base of one of the tentacles and label it *'thought'*.

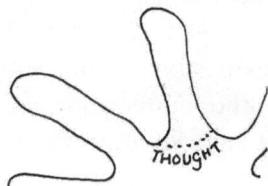

Then we were asked to draw an *eye* looking out from the upper part of the tentacle.

RIDING BACKWARDS ON AN OX, HE ENTERS THE BUDDHA HALL

T he Ox is a synonym for the mind.

Oxen are known to be stubborn and need to be well trained to be useful in work. It is a popular synonym in the East for the stubborn mind.

To achieve a well-trained mind doesn't mean that one will necessarily use it to travel backwards. On the contrary, most would use it to go forward – into the world of the senses and try to become world conquerors.

The riding backwards is *away* from the senses.

The 'space', beyond the 'dotted line' at the base of the tentacle of the Universal Octopus, is filled with *thoughts*. The tentacle, or extension, is not broken in any place. Thus, apart from the dotted line – it is not separate from the Source (it only *thinks* it is).

The Buddha Hall is a return to Source, crossing the 'dotted line' to *no thought*.

DIFFERENT TYPES OF OX

There are different types of Ox – "All animals are equal but some are more equal than others". The Ox needs to be tied to a stake and left until it *gives up* wanting to wander off. It then settles down where it is.

There are forty different kinds of Meditation Subjects for this work. If it is a kasina, then one will repeatedly bring it to the mind's eye until the acquired image appears – it takes a lot of perseverance.

For some Oxen this work is impossible. It means giving up wandering off for ever-sweeter, tastier green grass as experienced through the senses.

Others take a long time because of *karma* and *vipāka* (karma result) – they are just plodders, but they need to persevere.

Others of a more intelligent nature can experience the unconditioned more easily. The Buddha himself took how many countless lives being reborn a Bodhisattva? Even then, nearly thirty years of living a luxurious life, and then over six years searching and nearly dying. Then a whole night to break-through into the Dhamma.

However, for us it is somewhat easier because he left us a straight path – The Noble Eightfold Path, to follow. The Ox will always want to wander off from left to right but if one can keep on the path – *the end of the journey is assured.*

- *First there is the letting go of what has been grasped.*

- *Then there is the letting go of reaching out which is without any pain at all and very rapid.*

- *Then there is the letting go of even the slightest reaching out.*

(By that time the 'dotted line' has been reached and can be crossed over.)

THE BEST WAY TO GET OUT OF A LABYRINTH IS NOT TO ENTER IT

T he labyrinth is mental. It is made of thoughts. If one *stops* the thoughts, the labyrinth disappears.

If one finds oneself in a labyrinth, the way out is to stop thinking. It is essential to develop this capacity – to *train* the mind to *stop* at will.

Stop the mind and the world disappears.

When the mind is trained to stop entering labyrinths, it can be used to do something useful – just like a tool. Taken out when needed and put back again when the job is over.

However, even doing something useful can become a labyrinth *if* it is an indulgence. One would not know until a hindrance had appeared – a reaction of some sort to a comment, criticism, praise etc.

There is still the *'bhavāsava labyrinth'* present (the desire to become).

MAGIC LANTERN

Here is a simile to make it easier to understand. There is a Magic Lantern in a room projecting pictures on to a wall – by becoming immersed in the projection, the mind is trapped in a labyrinth.

The 'stopping thinking' is to switch off the Magic Lantern. Of course, this gives only temporary relief; as soon as it is switched on again – the mind gets lost in projections. But by being able switch it off, the mind can *look* and *see* what *is*, and what it will see are *all* the slides, the frames that were used to colour the light.

These frames or slides are the *latent tendencies* in the mind.

If they can be removed, then the Magic Lantern can be switched *on* when needed and will only let out clear light.

This clear light shows up what it touches *rather* than enabling the mind's projections to colour whatever is perceived.

NOTE A THOUGHT AS EARLY
AS POSSIBLE

All labyrinths start from something small – just like the oak tree began as an acorn. This something small is a *thought* – one tiny, invisible thought, when grasped after, is what grows into the myriad labyrinths of the sangsāra.

To help us track the process, the Buddha said, "Mind comes first". And he classified our experience of living in terms of the Five Khandhas:

1. Body *(rūpa-khandha)*
2. Feeling *(vedanā-khandha)*
3. Perception *(saññā-khandha)*
4. Habitual Tendencies *(sankhāra-khanda)*
5. Consciousness *(viññāna-khandha)*

Everything we experience can be fitted into this classification.

Our moment-to-moment work is to note a *thought* – as early as possible. To identify it, see its characteristics of *aniccā, dukkha* and *anattā*, and let it go.

Thoughts are facsimiles of our experiences of the world and mental impulses towards it. If we catch a thought early enough, label it correctly and let it go, this will interrupt the constant flow.

Labelling them correctly, seeing them for what they are – just thoughts – weakens our attachment to them and allows the mind to empty. They are like tennis balls being thrown back at us; from the point of view of karma, each tennis ball that comes back to us is one that we have thrown. If we *react* to one hitting us and pick it up to throw it back – we are creating *more* thought and in this way the supply will never be exhausted.

However, if the work of *noting* is continuously done – the time it takes will vary from person to person because of 'vipāka karma' (left over karma from the past). The mind will gradually subside and it will meet the *dotted line* that separates it from its Source. Then this dotted line needs to be crossed before mind can flow back into the Unconditioned State.

STRING OF BEADS

There are different ways of communication. There is the spoken word, the written word, sign language and, higher than these, telepathy.

Here is a sign:

Just looking at the drawing – we see a continuous row of circles, all separate but joined as a thread joins a row of beads.

These circles can represent each single thought moment, or could represent each lifetime – a life followed by a short break, then another, and so on, continuously...

What can be observed is that the 'continuing' is not like the continuity of a pipe – solid without gaps. It is not solid. There is a gap between each thought. If one were able to stay in the gap, the whole continuity would disappear.

If the circles represent *thoughts*, then wholesome good thoughts will take the chain *up*, unwholesome evil thoughts will take the chain *down*. Up and down is the general pattern when viewed over a long period of time for most beings.

Going back to the Universal Octopus drawing – can it be that the 'dotted line', that separates the tentacle from the Centre, is the 'string of beads'?

The tentacle must have begun with a small bulge – a beginning of curiosity, a moving out. This actual beginning, if ever there was one, is unknowable, untraceable.

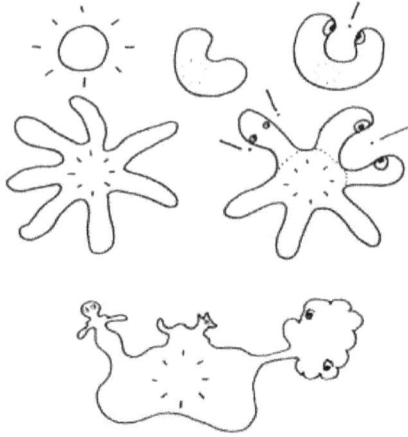

To satisfy the curiosity, the urge to explore, *senses* had to be created (even the amoeba has some sense contact). Thus the senses were created. The most highly developed sense for us all is visual. We have eyes - now everything can be seen!

But what is *seen* causes feelings of desire or fear because 'another', a something 'separate', is seen. From this – the whole of the sangsāra is created.

The *senses* can be closed off – in meditation the eyes are closed and the sense fields are closed down until all that is left is the mind and thoughts.

These thoughts, when examined, are made up of information from the senses. They flow on and on – the *past* being remembered, the *future* being planned, fantasies of both etc. etc.

By slowing down sense perception, the mind can be stopped from attaching to the objects of perception and the thoughts which arise – and withdraws from the sense doors to this 'dotted line' (or there is a rapid return to sense activity because the flow of thoughts is experienced as unbearable.)

It is the 'string of thoughts' that creates the idea of separateness.

There is in fact *no* break in the units of the circumference of the circle that represents the Unconditioned, *even* after IT has pushed out its many tentacles.

What this means is that in *reality* we are all ONE.

Whatever one is looking at is *oneself* reflected in myriad mirrors.

If this is seen – the adjustment to morality is spontaneous. If one hunts that 'other' – one is hunting *oneself*... If one does good to that 'other' – one is doing good to *oneself*... It means also that as there is only One Mind – the thoughts of 'others' can be known.

Yet, even when this is understood and people begin to live religious lives, still, the *feeling* of being separate has *not* been overcome. The 'string of beads', the 'dotted line' (the thoughts of separateness) has to be passed through for a return to Source – ending forever all separateness.

Then everything is understood, *life* and *death*, *karma* and the *sangsāra*.

SANKHĀRAS ARE ALL CREATED FROM THE PAST

W hat does the 'String of Beads', the 'Dotted Line', represent? It represents the sankhāras. Sankhāras are not easily understood. Descriptions given are long and usually written by academics who have *not* experienced them – only thought about them.

In Dependent Origination, Ignorance *(avijjā)* of the Four Noble Truths, of actual reality, is what *conditions* the *sankhāras.*

Sankhāras condition *consciousness.*

Consciousness conditions *nāma rūpa.*

Nāma Rūpa conditions the *six sense bases.*

The Six Sense Bases condition *contact.*

Contact conditions *feeling.*

Feeling conditions *craving.*

Craving conditions *clinging.*

Clinging conditions *becoming.*

Becoming conditions *birth, old age, sickness* and *death.*

Sankhāras are present *before* consciousness.

This means that they come from the *sub-conscious* which is out-of-sight, like a closed door. These sankhāras are all created from the *past* and bubble up out of the sub-conscious when *sensory contact* activates a similar sight, sound, smell etc. A stranger walking into a room can bring immediate *feelings* of attraction or aversion – coloured by the bubbling up of sankhāras which influence perception.

Something about the stranger reminds the sankhāras which then stain, as it were, *present* consciousness – colouring it with past impressions. This is going on all the time with everything.

HOW TO DEAL WITH THE
DOTTED LINE

S o, how to deal with this 'Dotted Line' – this 'String of Sankhāras' which separates one from the Unconditioned, the Source, Nibbāna?

One way is to try and deal with one sankhāra at a time. This is what you pay a psychiatrist to help you do. As there is no end to them, one sankhāra just leads to another, to another, to another – more and more labyrinths.

Another way is to get rid of them all at once. To just see them as single frames or slides that *consciousness* has been projecting through. But it is difficult to throw them *all* out and let go of *everything*. (Remember what it's like when clearing a loft or cupboard? Try to throw out all the stuff and mind thinks that maybe this will come in useful, and this... one is lost again in labyrinths.)

A third way is to stop the continuous flow of sankhāras by entering absorption – the Jhānas. This gives a taste of the Unconditioned, a taste of Nibbāna. It is also an excellent way of dealing with the sangsāra – to be able to control the mind at will and enter jhāna, experience bliss for ten minutes or whatever, and return refreshed, peaceful and happy.

From the jhānic state, one will be able to *dip* into the 'Source' and view the 'String of Sankhāras' from the other side – the inside! And this will make all the difference.

Jhānic states are only temporary cessation of sankhāras - the sankhāras are latent. When one stops meditating, however, they will be triggered off again.

So, the work is to investigate, understand, and *let go* of the sankhāras – for good.

This may take years, or lifetimes, but one is on the right track.

One just needs to persevere.

THE TWO LOKAS

The original meaning:

- LOKA. Noun: Space, emptiness; a world or plane of being.

- LOKYIA. Adjective: Worldly, mundane (as opposed to supramundane).

There are the *lokas* entirely constructed of *sankhāras*. Worlds of physical matter, mental form and formless worlds.

There is the unconditioned *loka* - which the Buddha described as:

"Truly, there is a loka, where there is neither earth, nor water, nor fire, nor air, nor the loka of infinite space, nor the loka of infinite consciousness, nor the loka of the void, nor the loka of neither perception nor non-perception; where there is no "this world" nor "other world"; neither moon nor sun.

This I call neither coming, nor going, nor standing still, nor being born, nor dying. There is neither fixity, nor movement, nor any base support. This is the end of suffering.

There is an unborn, a not-become, an uncreated, a not-compounded. If there were not this unborn, this not-become, this uncreated, this not-compounded, escape from the loka of the born, the become, the created, the compounded would not be possible.

But since there is an unborn, a not-become, an uncreated, a not-compounded, therefore there is an escape from the born, the become, the created, the compounded."

That is a 'loka' without sankhāras. Nibbāna.

If there were not this unconditioned world, said the Buddha, there could be no escape from the conditioned world in which suffering is experienced.

The jhānas, concentrated states of mental absorption with detachment from the world, have something of the taste of Nibbāna. If you can strive and experience these for yourself, you may adjust your style of life to become more contemplative and detached. (Or you may not; you may just use the bliss and extra power of concentration to have an easier, more successful worldly life.)

THE WORLD SEEMS NORMAL AND REAL

S itting in this room, everything seems very normal. I see people and furniture; out of the window I see the privet hedge, flowers and the sky. If I *touch* this world, this *loka* – it feels real. This table is hard, the carpet soft... Some of the things I think of as mine – *my* slippers, *my* reading glasses, *my* notebook...

Though the sun does light up the objects *seen*, the actual luminosity comes from within. It is a *livingness* that can reach through the *sense doors* and *know* this world. But the 'livingness' for all of us will one day come to an end. It is like a battery that eventually runs out, our *karma* runs out – and everything that we have taken as normal and real, disappears.

All the things that we have worked so hard to acquire; all our relationships, our bodies, our things – they disappear! Yet this is a busy *loka*, a busy world – everybody busy with what is eventually going to perish.

Is it worth it?

THERE BEING NO DUALITY, PLURALISM IS UNTRUE

The 'Two Lokas' is slightly misleading. If the Unconditioned is considered to be the Sea, and the conditioned the Wave – there is in reality, only Sea. The waves are just sea in motion.

'There being no duality, pluralism is untrue'.

What makes up the wave is thought.

When thinking *stops* – the wave disappears.

It is very, very difficult for beings to *stop* thinking. The mind needs to be tamed and trained. There needs to be understanding.

First of all, there needs to understanding of the conditioned world. We all have plenty of experience of it – but how much understanding? We need to understand the mind and how it works but not by reading books about it but through *direct experience* and *observation* of it.

What we find is that the world appears to be covered with a film of *desire*. The mind is constantly reaching out through desire and aversion.

The practice is to *let go.*

To let go of all thoughts, desires, memories of the past, planning, remembering and so on... To let go and let the mind settle to its natural, calm state which will give the experience of the Unconditioned – Nibbāna.

The *letting go* can be done by brute force or through understanding that there's *nothing* worth grasping after, or by a mix of the two.

Understanding is required - first of the conditioned world, secondly of the mind itself and then understanding of the *Unconditioned* will naturally arise.

HOW TO REACH THE UNCONDITIONED

It's very difficult to experience the *unconditioned* because we are immersed in the conditioned world – even though the unconditioned is present *now* and *everywhere*. This difficulty is because there is so much movement of thought.

We think the body is *ourself.* "*My* head hurts..." *My* hair is black..." etc. etc. Yet, the Buddha describes the body as being a *puppet*, a dead thing – just a collection of elements. The strings that pull the puppet are at the sense doors and the volition is *desire* from the mind.

There is *matter* and *mind.*

The only worlds we know are through the sense doors - the six worlds of *seeing, hearing, tasting, smelling, touching* and *thinking.* A being may have only one sense of touch, others only two or three. If we lose one sense e.g. *sight* - the whole world of sight is lost to us.

It may be a long and tedious process to reach the unconditioned, but it need not be so.

There are *two ways* of reaching it:

1) Through Concentration, which is fine if you can develop good concentration. One just passes through all the conditioned states of happiness and bliss seeing it's '*Not this...*' '*Not this...*' until one reaches Nibbāna.

2) The other way is through Understanding. If, for example, I'm in a restaurant and there is a plate of food in front of me. I can use concentration and determination to resist the food and am able to walk out of the restaurant. The mind just controls with *'Not this...'* *'Not this...'* and moves on and out. However, using understanding one sits and looks at the plate of food, really *looks* and *sees* only maggots and worms. It would be easy to let go of wanting anything on that plate and get up and leave.

So, we examine the world through *sankhāras* and see that everything is just made up of bits which will fall apart. Seeing it this way, nothing is worth grasping after.

Then we examine the world through the *Universal Octopus* with the tentacles, which, though not separate, appear to be cut off from the Centre, the Source, by a 'dotted line' – a string of sankhāras, which is only movement of thought.

We try to experience the *unconditioned* and meet difficulties. The difficulties are in one's own mind! One needs to turn *inwards* and learn to control and understand this mind. The point is not to be concerned with others' faults but to look inwards and *know* what is going on inside one's own mind.

Control and *understand* your own mind.

KNOW NIBBĀNA EXISTS

W hy do we want to control and understand the mind? Is it to have a more peaceful and easier time in the sangsāra?

To be more useful in the world?

To get rid of suffering?

Or is it to attain the highest understanding, Nibbāna – the unconditioned state?

How the Buddha puts it in the Four Noble Truths is to put an *end to suffering*. Suffering is the First Noble Truth.

The Third Noble Truth is that there *is* something marvellous and wonderful that can be realised and found *within* ourselves. The extraordinary thing is that as one tries to locate 'IT', imagine say by knocking on a door – 'IT' knocks back!

The Buddha didn't describe 'IT' rather he described what it was not, so as to avoid conceptual thinking getting in the way. Those who read about another's experience of this *Source, God, One Mind, Tao, Emptiness, Nibbāna...* can get stuck in conceptual thinking about it and never experience 'IT' for themselves.

Call it God, Nibbāna, One... it's *not* the name. It's there to be realised but is blocked out because of filters. Suspend disbelief and know that Nibbāna exists and is better than the best we could ever *experience* as humans.

PART II

THE NOBLE EIGHTFOLD PATH

Right Understanding

Right Thought

Right Speech

Right Action

Right Livelihood

Right Effort

Right Mindfulness

Right Concentration

WHAT DO YOU WANT?

The unexpected and serious question *"What do you want?"* elicited a range of answers including:

"I would like to have Right View permanently in place..."

"I would like to be always happy..."

"I would like to continue working with the Noble Eightfold Path to see where it will take me..."

"I would like to always do good deeds..."

"I would like to be happy and useful..."

It is obvious from your replies that no one answered "Nibbāna". Though you may think that you are following the Noble Eightfold Path, your answers suggest that the goal of your *true* inner framework is different from the goal of the Noble Eightfold Path.

If it's not the Noble Eightfold Path – it is a path of putting fuel on the fire.

What is happening is that you are still trying to stick the Noble Eightfold Path on to something else – on to your *desires*. As a result, there is no change, no progress on the Path.

The Path needs to come from *within* and change you. Otherwise, all you are doing is putting on an overcoat, putting on a top hat and beard, putting on a front... The *kilesas* involved are deceit, hypocrisy, laziness, pretentiousness, pride…

At death it's too late to be serious, too late to say, *"If only…"*. Most die in pain. This affects the mind. *"He's gone…"* they say. Then after shuffling the body off somewhere and tidying up whatever mess one has left, they might feel sad, glad, or indifferent – and carry on with their lives.

The change to become serious has to begin *now*.

To have the right *goal* that ends all unsatisfactory states, is peaceful and happy – Nibbāna.

OBNOSIS

O bnosis means 'seeing the obvious'.

It's easy to see the faults in others but not in oneself. There is an old Thai saying: *"If it comes out of other people, we say it smells bad. If it comes out of ourselves, we say it smells nice!"*

Habit energy is very strong.

The castle walls have been built to protect and stop anything entering. To break them down would mean a *threat* to survival – and one wishes to survive.

These walls were built to stop further pain, to protect an 'old wound', and behavior patterns have developed to 'cover-up' this wound.

One has no intention of allowing the walls to be dismantled and thus enable a *change* in behavior as it might mean a glimpse of the pain one is protecting oneself from. Thus, one refuses to use obnosis *(seeing the obvious)* on oneself.

POINT OF VIEW

P oints of view change. In themselves they have very little energy. Like an arrow, they need a 'bow' to give them energy and direction.

Feelings arise and give *energy* to points of view.

We think this is going on *inside* us, but the moment we observe that it is *outside* – there is a spontaneous detachment and a severing forever of the power of *feeling* to manipulate one's responses.

MOST JUST DRIFT ALONG

An elephant was considered trained when it was prepared to lose its life in battle following commands. How many people have trained themselves in this way?

Most just drift along as *effects* to causes they are *not* conscious of. They get blown about by the winds of karma.

These 'causes' arise in the subconscious part of the mind and are the *latent tendencies* of the past.

DRIFTING ALONG WITH UNCONSCIOUS FRAMEWORKS

The unseen, unconscious inner framework common to most is one of survival – fight or run.

Other frameworks are the desire for power, the desire to mate, the desire for pleasure… These desires create frameworks that are not consciously put into place.

The drifting along with *unconscious frameworks* with one at effect is very dangerous and unsatisfactory.

When one wakes up to this (if only for a brief time), one looks around for a *conscious framework* in some faith or religion. This is the beginning of taking the reins into your own hands, of trying to become the cause rather than effect.

INNER FRAMEWORKS LEAVE FOOTPRINTS

T hese inner frameworks leave footprints of two kinds: The first in *response* to some inner or outer phenomena: like the fulfillment of a desire (*wholesome or unwholesome*). The second type of footprint is of the *reactive* mind: the way the mind reacts to a sudden unexpected situation.

Is it from a *conscious* framework? Or from the *subconscious;* an old root from the past?

There needs to be *one* framework to deal with *both* kinds. The old roots need to be dug out. The desires need to *consciously* arise from a true framework – not some old framework dragging you along.

Unsound ways of dealing with the 'old roots' are alcohol, barbiturates, change of environment and concentration – because they are only temporary.

The cure needs to be permanent.

A CONSCIOUS FRAMEWORK
NEEDS TO BE PROTECTED

T he Romans always built a defense before camping or building. This is what we need to do – build a *defense* mechanism with the mind that protects the conscious framework.

To *catch* the aberrations as soon as they arise and not let them grow, become unmanageable, and take control of our *thoughts, speech* and *actions*, thus becoming, yet again, the effect instead of the cause.

To have a defense mechanism that acts in the moment and *stops* the spilling over of *kilesas* into thoughts, speech and deeds.

This is what we need. Thus the building of a *new* framework is required to do this.

The framework must have a goal. The Noble Eightfold Path's goal is the highest happiness – Nibbāna. (When this goal is attained, the framework is no longer needed, it disappears.)

WHAT CONTROLS THE MIND?

T he 'horse and rider' is a metaphor for the mind and what 'drives' it. The mind is 'not self', and it is not controlled by you – it is controlled by the kilesas.

To take control of the mind, the kilesas *(defilements)* need to be overcome. They take the horse all over the place and only 'you' have to suffer.

The mind needs just as much clearing up as it has been messed up and neglected. Neglected 80% needs 80% tidied up. It's like travelling five hundred miles from home; it's five hundred miles to get back *if* you manage to keep to a direct route.

Along the way, one is trying to gain control of the mind.

This is the job that needs to be done, to *understand* and *control* the mind.

KNOW YOUR FRAMEWORK

W hat comes before desire is viewpoint. Something has to be seen, heard, tasted, smelt, touched, thought and viewed as being desirable; therefore viewed as being permanent and conducive to happiness.

Returning to frameworks – the usual frameworks are made for survival, pursuit of pleasure and pursuit of power.

It's a good thing if one keeps the Five Precepts. That puts one on a very high level as a human being. However, it's not enough. Not enough to deal with the problem of suffering as the Buddha saw suffering: *Birth, Death, Old Age, Sickness, Unhappy Mental States...*

These unhappy mental states are hot. They are burning with passions. One's framework should be able to cool them, cool them down and let them go out. *(Or put them out with Dhamma water.)*

One shouldn't put petrol on the fire.

Without knowing your framework, you are just blown about by the winds of karma. One also needs to know the goals of these frameworks e.g. when there is a feeling of being attacked – which framework responds? Usually survival: *"You push me, I push you..."*

To understand that most of your supposed needs and wants, and that most of the apparently useful things you do are done out of *"I want..."* from an old, not very highly developed framework that arises moment to moment.

They change as they are *effects* rather than causes.

If we haven't the Noble Eightfold Path framework in place *all* the time – it is because we haven't suffered enough. A hungry man has the goal to feed himself; he finds the food and knows the goal is accomplished.

THERE IS NO IDENTITY

T he six senses are neutral. The eye is neutral, the eye object and seeing consciousness are all neutral. They are a cause-and-effect phenomenon.

The *eye* is just like a window into the world. I need the window to see into the garden; the window is completely neutral; it just facilitates seeing.

What changes it from being neutral is the *mind*.

The Noble Eightfold Path gets tacked on to one's old habitual tendencies and latent ones. It doesn't and cannot, therefore, *change* one. It must come from *within* and become a new way of living, seeing, thinking… This is where the problem lies.

Your problems lie in grasping after *identities*, grasping after roles to play.

There is no identity.

Those who discover this by accident using drugs or some external aid go mad. But fortunately, this should not happen within a Buddhist framework.

The Buddha tells us how to speak, think, conduct ourselves etc. not as something to identify with; it's a training of something that has been neglected for a long time. A training of something that is *'not self'*.

IRON FILINGS AND MAGNETS

J umping from a 'bedroom window' is a type of karma that cannot be put right. There is a moment of standing on the window frame, the safety of the room behind you; you can choose to step back into the house but once, out of *free* choice, you jump – all freedom is lost.

You are now at the mercy of all the bigger magnets.

If you are not in control of the mind, it's like a horse without training; it will take you all over the place, rolling in mud etc. and you will have to go along with it.

What is attracted to the 'bigger magnets' are the 'iron filings' in your mind. If there were only a very few, or even one, the big magnets of the world would not have much pull on you. But if there are lots – you get drawn all over the place.

The basic Buddhist practice *is 'Don't do bad, do good and purify the mind'.* This work of *purifying* the mind is to remove all the 'iron filings' from the mind.

All the latent tendencies.

These 'iron filings' take the form of thoughts, feelings, ideas…

FREEDOM TO
OR FREEDOM FROM?

'Freedom to'... becomes meaningless if there's nothing you want freedom to *do*. It's the same with 'freedom from...' if there is nothing you want freedom *from*. It means that one is content wherever one is and therefore – free.

What comes before 'freedom to...' is *wanting*.

What comes before 'freedom from...' is *wanting*.

It's like the alcoholic or drinker wants freedom to drink; he also wants freedom from a hangover. He therefore looks for a pill or something to cure the hangover. Great effort goes into producing something that satisfies people's wanting freedom from the results of some of the things people get up to.

The way to 'free up' this *wanting* would be to *stop* putting fuel on the fire.

STOP PUTTING FUEL ON THE FIRE

E ach of us has something that we *do* that gives unsatisfactory results.

It's difficult to be objective about ourselves. Feelings and thoughts continually obscure our objectivity and honesty. But if we could just catch that moment when the hand goes out to grasp and *stop* it – we would free ourselves from the resultant unsatisfactoriness that we don't want.

- To note a familiar mental pattern emerging.

- To trace it back to where it began.

- To see where it is heading—

- and stop it!

IMAGES

The main point to understand about an *image* is that it is just a copy. It is not the real thing.

To project an image that you have certain attributes which you do not, in fact, have is a deception. It is an intention to deceive because you want something. Examples include a 'boy' pretends to be a 'hero' to attract the girls – when they find out that he isn't a 'hero', they find him repulsive.

It's not always bad to create a good and wholesome image and try to live up to it. That is different from pretending you are already the good and wholesome image.

It is possible to build up your good attributes and remove the unwholesome ones. The Buddha talked of beings who had done this as being *'Brahma become'*. The main thing is to persevere, to prioritise and actually put the Buddha's teaching into practice.

SOMEONE WHO
HAS SUFFERED ENOUGH

I t is good karma to have an excellent book. Bad karma if you don't read it or understand it.

It is good karma to be *"...a young man from a good family."*

It is good karma to have *"...suffered enough."*

There are two things that happen to someone who has suffered enough, just like someone who has been tortured and finally has had enough. They say, "Stop! I want the suffering to stop!" And they ask, "Why am I suffering?"

This leads to a genuine investigation of the Four Noble Truths. The Third Noble Truth : the stopping of suffering *(Nibbāna),* and the First Noble Truth : the acknowledgement of suffering, are the answers.

The "Why?" leads to the Second Noble Truth which is : grasping. The way to *'let go'* is the Fourth Noble Truth : the Noble Eightfold Path.

Because it is now an urgent genuine investigation, the results will be genuine. Even if it takes lifetimes, one will *know* that one is on the right path and slowly make progress – slowly collecting life's jigsaw pieces to complete one's understanding of the *sangsāra.*

DE-ACTIVATING THE SUB-CONSCIOUS

It is true that the subconscious *(bhavanga)* is a storehouse of all past actions, feelings, thoughts etc. and that it is activated by sense contact. Then something 'pops up' and creates more karma - because it was grasped after.

It 'pops up' as *feelings, perceptions* and *thoughts* and these are constantly *grasped* after, creating more karma and re-filling the storehouse of rubbish and debris from the past.

To de-activate it, one needs to stop grasping, stop desire, stop the *āsava* - the desire to become *(bhavāsava),* and it will subside and disappear, no longer causing rebirth again in the sangsāra.

Question: *"If the subconscious disappears, how was the Buddha able to recall and remember past events and lifetimes?"*

Answer: *"The memory can be contactable just like opening a filing cabinet to find a particular file. The Buddha could do that, use the relevant information required at the present moment and then let it go. There was no rummaging around, bumping into this and that, and becoming associative.*

Someone who has completed the work can use the memory bank which doesn't exist anywhere but can arise in a given moment and will disappear when not required – nothing clung to."

THERE IS NO OTHER

I t is true that everything in the world is in a state of evolution – a state of evolution towards understanding.

As there is unity, this movement is towards balance to try and bring about understanding. It has a pendulum-type effect – thus there are Hell Realms that are full of beings who are experiencing just what they did to another.

This suffering is to teach that *'what one does to another one is doing to oneself'* as, in truth, there is no 'other'.

It is only through ignorance that separate, individual selves are created. Because of wrong understanding, they *think* of themselves as autonomous. They suffer. They feel lonely. They feel separate.

What the stories of the seven-year-olds who became *Arahats* in the time of the Buddha, and the king's minister who became a *Paccekabuddha* on seeing a leaf fall from a tree, and the realization that arises from the practice of *Satipatthana,* have in common is - *understanding.*

With understanding comes spontaneous adjustment.

The seven-year-olds, having just joined the *Sangha,* would not have too much of an adjustment to make as the Aryan Way of life was the norm for monks. But the king's minister just left. Without leaving a note – he just flew away to the Himalayas!

WHAT ARE YOU THINKING NOW?

Recollection of remembering to note what one's mind is thinking about enables the removal of negative thoughts.

Mind comes first.

If all the negative thoughts like *"I can't..."* were removed, that leaves all the room for positive thoughts – thus anything is possible.

We are all the product of the past. The present moment is creating the future. We can create whatever future we desire in the present moment – now.

What are you thinking now?

There is karma and resultant karma *(vipāka karma)*. The past karma is what makes up the present. It would seem to condition the future – but it need not be so.

If the present karma was allowed to just burn itself out – without any new fuel added to it, the future would become free of the past. The past would become latent. Of course, it doesn't absolutely disappear, it can be recalled when needed – but it no longer conditions the mind.

By continually monitoring the mind all the negative thoughts can be filtered out, including the subtle, to the very subtle forms of *greed, ill will* and *delusion*.

It is through continual mindfulness that we gain control of the mind and stop its wavering, out of control, habitual tendency. By filtering out the negative thoughts we can use positive thoughts to create the future we desire.

This can only be done NOW - in the present moment.

The past has gone and can be let go. The future has not come. Only the present moment is real.

(Those who have a lot of bad karma from the past find thoughts dwelling there and have difficulty being in the present moment – the past is too weighty.)

HE WHO PRACTISES THE DHAMMA IS HAPPY!

There is a reason for everything. From a Buddhist point of view there are two reasons for doing meditation.

The first is because it makes one happy. One finds a level of happiness that is higher than any happiness that has been experienced in the pursuit of pleasure through sense gratification (or from creating good karma).

The second is to realize Truth. To *penetrate* Dhamma by which the supreme level of happiness is attained.

One needs to clarify the reason why one meditates. Is it for one or both the right reasons? (Or is it because one has been told to? Or because it is time to meditate and it has just become a habit?)

One needs to experience the results of *happiness* or increased *understanding* (and not just a short doze or an uncomfortable body).

MY LIFE

sn't it amazing that a seed will grow into exactly
what's on the picture of a seed packet whether it's in
English, Scottish or Thai soil?   It will shape the
elements into e.g. a geranium.

Most beings are like the example of the 'geranium'.   Mind
has shaped them from the elements at birth and most grow
up into what they were born into.   Yet, unlike the
geranium – a human being can change.

The mind can be freed from *identification* with its human
form and can choose to be a Brahma, or a Deva, or to
attain one of the Four Stages of Sainthood.

It can do this by, moment to moment, in the *present*,
consciously choosing to mould *thoughts, speech* and
actions to the Noble Eightfold Path, and by awareness and
investigation developing *understanding*.

Only man is free to do this but how far have any of us
got?   The moment of Death is sudden and unexpected –
what will our last thought moment be?

SLOWING DOWN THE MIND

M y 'life' is made up of time. *"Time is its own place..."* There is the time of clocks and the sun moving round a stick – but the mind has its own time.

Time can pass slowly or very quickly. The mind can be made consciously to slow things down. Through mindfulness and observation, time can appear to be slowed down. (Just as the physical can be speeded up through movement to move so fast as to disappear as the elements fall apart and disintegrate.)

In this slowing down, what is seen is that *mind* and *matter* are separate.

Matter seems to be like a mirrored reflection in the mind, and the mind becomes *involved* with it. If this 'involvement' is *stopped*, it becomes apparent that they are separate.

The *mind* can still affect *matter* and move it around. Just as matter can become enmeshed with mind by the mind identifying with it.

In this comprehension of mind and matter being separate – there is a *power*. The power of being able, mentally, to reconstruct matter. This can occur when the mental process has been slowed down so much that it is easy to understand *how* to manipulate matter with mind.

This can cause an explosion of self-power: the āsava – *bhavāsava*. But with right understanding of the *three characteristics,* this obstacle should be avoided.

MAKING LISTS

I t is true that these lists of the main tenets within Buddhism offer a picture of the philosophy of Buddhism but their main purpose is to make one into a real Buddhist.

Someone who is interested in cars will patiently sit by the side of the road to spot them: "There goes an Aston Martin, a Vauxhall, a Roll Royce, a Mercedes..." and so on.

Someone who is interested in butterflies learns their names and can spot them wherever he is; Cornwall, Wales, Ireland, Scotland etc. and he labels them; "Fritillary, Cabbage White, Yellow Emperor, Peacock..." and so on. Some are very common. Some are very rare.

We need to see the butterfly thoughts in the mind, spot them, and label them correctly. To label divine wholesome thoughts; *Sympathetic Joy, Compassion, Loving Kindness, Equanimity* and note the good feeling it gives the mind. To particularly label the poisonous spider type thoughts; *envy, resentment, anger...* and root them out.

Sometimes they come in clouds of butterfly-type thoughts but still they *need* to be identified. This way, one gains control of one's thoughts.

To be really interested in one's thoughts is essential, and to monitor them all the time. If we don't spot the butterfly-thought, it will cause karma to be created without our conscious control – and we will be heirs to that karma.

- Use the lists to remind you of the different types of thoughts.

- Check out that you understand the meaning.

- Make a practical use of these lists in Buddhism—

- *and* become a real Buddhist.

APPENDIX

Some Lists of the Main Tenets within Buddhism

TEN KARMICALLY WHOLESOME ACTIONS

1. Right understanding of karma. ⎤
2. Absence of covetousness.   **MENTAL ACTION**
3. Absence of ill will. ⎦
4. To abstain from lying. ⎤
5. To abstain from tale-bearing.   **VERBAL ACTION**
6. To abstain from harsh language. ⎢
7. To abstain from frivolous talk. ⎦
8. To abstain from killing. ⎤
9. To abstain from stealing.   **BODILY ACTION**
10. To abstain from sexual misconduct. ⎦

TEN KARMICALLY UNWHOLESOME ACTIONS

1. Wrong understanding of karma. ⎤
2. Covetousness   **MENTAL ACTION**
3. Ill will. ⎦
4. False speech. ⎤
5. Slandering.   **VERBAL ACTION**
6. Harsh talk. ⎢
7. Frivolous talk. ⎦
8. Taking away life of living beings. ⎤
9. Taking what is not given.   **BODILY ACTION**
10. Sexual misconduct. ⎦

TEN KUSALA KAMMA
(Merit Making Actions)

1. Charity *(dāna)*
2. Morality *(sīla)*
3. Mental culture *(bhāvanā)*
4. Respect for Elders and Parents
5. Service
6. Transference of merit to others
7. Rejoicing in others' merits *(anumuditā)*
8. Hearing the Dhamma
9. Teaching the Dhamma
10. Forming correct views

TEN PĀRAMI
(Perfections)

1. Generosity *(dāna)*
2. Morality *(sīla)*
3. Desirelessness *(nekkhama)*
4. Wisdom *(paññā)*
5. Energy *(viriya)*
6. Patience *(khanti)*
7. Truthfulness *(sacca)*
8. Determination *(adhiṭṭhāna)*
9. Loving Kindness *(mettā)*
10. Equanimity *(upekkhā)*

THE FIVE BUDDHIST PRECEPTS
(pañca-sīla)

1. I undertake to observe the precept to abstain from killing living beings.
   (Pānātipātā veramanī-sikkhāpadam samādiyāmi)

2. I undertake to observe the precept to abstain from taking things not given.
   (Adinnādānā veramanī-sikkhāpadam samādiyāmi)

3. I undertake to observe the precept to abstain from sexual misconduct.
   (Kāmesu micchācārā veramanī-sikkhāpadam samādiyāmi)

4. I undertake to observe the precept to abstain from false speech.
   (Musāvādā veramanī-sikkhāpadam samādiyāmi)

5. I undertake to observe the precept to abstain from intoxicating drinks and drugs causing heedlessness.
   (Surāmeraya - majja - pamādaṭṭhānā veramanī-sikkhāpadam samādiyāmi)

TEN KILESAS
(defilements)

1. Greed *(lobha)*

2. Hate *(dosa)*

3. Delusion *(moha)*

4. Conceit *(māna)*

5. Opinionated Views *(diṭṭhi)*

6. Sceptical Doubt *(vicikicchā)*

7. Mental Torpor *(thīna)*

8. Restlessness *(uddhacca)*

9. Shamelessness *(ahirika)*

10. Lack of Moral Dread *(anottappa)*

LATENT TENDENCIES
(anusaya)

1. Sensuous Greed *(kāma-rāga)*
2. Grudge *(patigha)*
3. Speculative Opinion *(diṭṭhi)*
4. Uncertainty *(vicikicchā)*
5. Conceit *(māna)*
6. Craving for Existence *(bhava-rāga)*
7. Ignorance *(avijjā)*

TEN FETTERS
(samyojana)

1. Own Body Views *(sakkāya-diṭṭhi)*

2. Doubt *(vicikiccha)*

3. Clinging to the Practice of Morality *(sīlabbata-parāmāsa)*

4. Desire for Sense Objects *(kāma-rāga)*

5. Ill Will *(vyāpāda)*

6. Desire for Form *(rūpa-rāga)*

7. Desire for Formless Existence *(arūpa-rāga)*

8. Conceit *(māna)*

9. Restlessness *(uddhacca)*

10. Ignorance *(avijjā)*

FIVE HINDRANCES
(nivarana)

1. Ill Will *(vyāpāda)*
2. Greed *(kamacchanda)*
3. Doubt *(vicikicchā)*
4. Sloth and Torpor *(thīna-middha)*
5. Restlessness and Worry *(uddhacca-kukkucca)*

FOUR FOUNDATIONS OF MINDFULNESS *(satipaṭṭhāna)*

Body   *(kāyānupassanā satipaṭṭhāna)*
Feeling   *(vedanānupassanā satipaṭṭhāna)*
Mind   *(cittānupassanā satipaṭṭhāna)*
Dhammas *(dhammānupassanā satipaṭṭhāna)*

FIVE KHANDHAS
(Groups of Existence)

Corporeality *(rūpa)*
Feeling *(vedanā)*
Perception (*saññā)*
Mental Formations *(saṅkhāra)*
Consciousness *(viññāna)*

THE THREE CHARACTERISTICS
(*ti-lakkhana)*

All formations are Impermanent.
(sabbe saṅkhārā aniccā)
All formations are Unsatisfactory.
(sabbe saṅkhārā dukkha)
All things are without any kind of a Self.
(sabbe dhammā anattā)

ĀSAVAS
(cankers)

Sense Desire *(kāmāsava)*
Desire for Existence *(bhavāsava)*
Wrong Views *(diṭṭhāsava)*
Ignorance *(avijjāsava)*

THE FOUR NOBLE TRUTHS
(ariya-sacca)

1. The Noble Truth of Suffering (*dukkha*).

2. The Noble Truth of the Origin of Suffering (*dukkha–samudaya*).

3. The Noble Truth of the Extinction of Suffering (*dukkha– nirodha*).

4. The Noble Truth of the Path that leads to the Extinction of Suffering (*dukkha–nirodh–gāmini–paṭipadā)*.

FOUR BRAHMA-VIHĀRAS
(Divine Abodes)

Loving Kindness *(mettā)*
Compassion *(karunā)*
Sympathetic Joy *(muditā)*
Equanimity *(upekkhā)*

FOUR ROADS TO SUCCESS
(iddhi-pāda)

Zeal *(chanda)*
Energy *(viriya)*
Will *(citta = mind, consciousness)*
Investigation *(vimamsa)*

SPIRITUAL
FACULTIES and POWERS
(Five Indriya and Five Bala)

Confidence *(saddā)*
Energy *(viriya)*
Mindfulness *(sati)*
Concentration *(samādhi)*
Wisdom *(paññā)*

THE FOUR ELEMENTS
(dhātu)

Earth *(pathavi-dhātu)*
Fire *(tejo-dhātu)*
Air *(vāyo-dhātu)*
Water *(āpo-dhātu)*

SEVEN FACTORS OF ENLIGHTENMENT
(bojjhanga)

1. Mindfulness *(sati)*
2. Investigation of the Truth *(dhamma-vicaya)*
3. Energy *(viriya)*
4. Rapture *(pīti)*
5. Tranquillity *(passāddhi)*
6. Concentration *(samādhi)*
7. Equanimity *(upekkhā)*

THE FOUR SAMPAJAÑÑAS
(comprehensions)

1. Speak only what is *USEFUL.* When about to say something… use wise discrimination, will it be useful or not? *(satthaka-sampajañña)*

2. Speak only what is *SUITABLE.* Even if useful… use wise discrimination, is it suitable or not? *(sappāya-sampajañña)*

3. Note without letting up the *PHYSICAL* and *MENTAL PHENOMENA* that keep arising. *(gocara-sampajañña)*

4. Understand without delusion how *IMPERMANENT,* subject to *SUFFERING,* and lacking a *SELF* are *all* phenomena. *(asammoha-sampajañña)*

THE NOBLE EIGHTFOLD PATH
(*ariya-aṭṭhangika-magga*)

1. Right Understanding
   (sammā-diṭṭhi)

2. Right Thought
   (sammā-sañkappa)

3. Right Speech
   (sammā-vācā)

4. Right Action
   (sammā-kammanta)

5. Right Livelihood
   (sammā-ājīva)

6. Right Effort
   (sammā-vāyāma)

7. Right Mindfulness
   (sammā-sati)

8. Right Concentration
   (sammā-samādhi)

PRACTICAL GOOD CONDUCT
(saddhammas)

Generosity *(dāna)*
Morality *(sīla)*
Meditation *(bhāvanā)*

NOBLE CONDUCT
(carana-dhammas)

1. Morality *(sīla)*

2. Watching over the sense doors *(indrya-samvara)*

3. Moderation in eating *(bhojanemattaññutā)*

4. Wakefulness *(jāgariyanuyoga)*

5. Faith *(saddhā)*

6. Mindfulness *(sati)*

7. Moral shame *(hiri)*

8. Moral dread *(ottoppa)*

9. Great learning *(bahusacca)*

10. Energy *(vīriya)*

11. Wisdom *(paññā)*

12. – 15. Four Absorptions *(Four Jhānas)*

GLOSSARY OF PALI WORDS

Arahat: One who has got rid of ten fetters. He has realized Nibbāna in himself and will not be reborn.

TEN FETTERS:

1. Own body views.
2. Doubt.
3. Clinging to morality.
4. Craving for sense objects and existence.
5. Ill will.
6. Craving for form (fine material) existence.
7. Craving for formless existence.
8. Conceit. Pride.
9. (Mental) Restlessness.
10. Ignorance.

The first five bind to the lower worlds. The second five bind to the higher worlds.

Āsavas: Desire for sensual existence. There are three, sometimes four: Desire for Becoming; Desire for Sense Objects; Views and Opinions; Ignorance.

Avijjā: Not seeing. Ignorance of the Four Noble Truths concerning Suffering; its Cause; its Cessation; The Way leading to its Cessation.

Asmi-māna: The conceit that I Am (a separate entity).

Upādāna: Clinging; an intensified result of craving. Before one has something, one *craves* for it. When one gets it, one *clings* to it.

Brahma-Vihāras: Dwelling places of Brahma. Sublime (Divine) states of mind: Friendliness, Compassion, Sympathetic Joy and Equanimity. Together, they produce an attitude of mind towards all other beings which is wholly positive and beneficial.

Dāna: Giving, generosity. A fundamental virtue and intentional practice.

Pāli: An Indo-European language related to Sanskrit in which the Buddha taught and in which the suttas were later recorded.

Paticca-samuppāda: Dependent Origination.

Avijjā (Ignorance) forms the base for *Sañkhāras.*
Sañkhāras forms the base for *Consciousness.*
Consciousness forms the base for *Mind and Body.*
Mind and Body form the base for the *Six Sense Bases.*
The Six Sense Bases forms the base for *Contact.*
Contact forms the base for *Feeling.*
Feeling forms the base for *Craving.*
Craving forms the base for *Clinging.*
Clinging forms the base for *Becoming.*
Becoming forms the base for *Birth.*
Birth forms the base for *Old Age, Sickness and Death.*

Dhamma: (Sanskrit: Dharma)
     1. Things.
     2. The Buddha's Teaching. The Truth.

Khandas: Groups, categories. The Buddha analyses our experiences into five categories: body, feeling, perception, sañkhāras and consciousness.

Kamma: (Sanskrit Karma): Action; Doing. Specifically how all actions have a cause and an effect and the relationship between them.

Jhānas: Tranquil meditative states in which the mind is withdrawn into itself, free of the five senses.

Māra: The Deity ruling over the Highest Heaven of the Sensuous Sphere. He tries to keep living beings enslaved in sensual existence, tempting all those who try to go beyond this, so that they fall back within his realm. For the six years before Buddha's Enlightenment and one year after it, he followed the Buddha, trying to find a weakness in him that he could exploit. He tried to persuade the Buddha to pass away into Parinibbāna without teaching the Dhamma. When the time came for the Buddha's Parinibbāna, he reappeared to urge him on. Immediately after the Buddha's death, Māra searched for some trace of him on earth and in the various heaven worlds without success.

Nāma-rūpa: Mind and Body. A Form and the Name given to it by humans.

Nibbāna: (Sanskrit Nirvāṇa). Every thing in the universe is a saṅkhāra. Nibbāna is not a saṅkhāra. Nibbāna is like the cinema screen. The universe is all the pictures and images superimposed on the screen. Because of the pictures, we can't see the screen. Yet it is there all the time. If we could clear the screen of the pictures, we would see it immediately. If we stop all sense perceptions and thoughts and images, Nibbāna is revealed. When we find the whole universe, mind and body, unsatisfactory, and let them go, they fall away from us and we experience total Peace and Happiness.

This is a state that has always been there. From time to time we get flashes of it. It is not death. Death is the end of something. Nibbāna is not the end of anything. It is a state without a beginning and without an end.

Sangsāra: The wandering on. The continuous process of being born, growing old, suffering and dying, in which beings are trapped. In its flow, they act and experience the consequences of their actions (Kamma). It embraces the whole spectrum of existence from the highest heavens to the lowest hells. Only the attainment of Nibbāna puts an end to the wandering.

Sammuti-sacca: Conventional truth. The whole fabric of our social lives as civilised or semi-civilised human beings and the roles we play in our public and private lives. As Shakespeare expressed it:

> *All the world's a stage,*
> *And all the men and women merely players;*
> *They have their exits and their entrances,*
> *And one man in his time plays many parts...*

So, we take up positions and play accepted parts in the social fabric, almost on a "let's pretend" basis (which is what 'sammuti' basically means). The parts are innumerable: policemen, teachers, politicians, doctors, carpenters, fathers, mothers, schoolchildren, labourers, - even soldiers. (Although if we choose to play at soldiers, we may find ourselves actually killing somebody, which suggests that the "game" might have got out of hand.)

Sankhāra: Something which is made up of parts; a compound. Not an unchanging thing in itself. Everything in the universe is a sankhāra. For example, a motor car; the parts come together and it exists; we can drive it. After a while, the parts fall apart and are reused or decay or are destroyed and there is nothing left over. For example, a human being.

We give things names, but once they have disintegrated into their respective parts, there is nothing left over to correspond to the name.

Mental things are also sankhāras. Thoughts come into existence, based on perception, then they disappear. They form parts of trains of thought, which in their turn break up and vanish.

The sangsāra is made up of sankhāras. Just as the moving picture on the screen is made up of images of people, cities, trees etc.

Nibbāna is not a sankhāra, just as the screen is not in any way a part of the film and its images.

Sankhāras depend on Ignorance of the Four Noble Truths. Once the truth about suffering is realised, ignorance disappears. Just as when the screen is seen, we no longer believe in the reality of the film.

Sīla: Morality, right behaviour. The basis of morality is not causing suffering to oneself or others. Particularly, *one should not do to others what one doesn't like being done to oneself.*

Sotāpanna: A "stream enterer". One who has entered the stream of activity which leads to Nibbāna. He has put an end to the first three Fetters.

Sutta: Discourse by the Buddha himself or certain of his leading disciples.

Tanhā: Craving. The cause of suffering. Literally it means "thirst". If one thinks of the thirst of an alcoholic for alcohol, one gets some idea of the strength of the term. So long as there is craving for anything whatsoever, good or bad, one will always be motivated to enter into a form of existence where the object of one's craving can be found.

Upādāna-khanda: Clinging to the five khandas which make up the whole of a human being's life: body, feelings, perceptions, thoughts (sañkhāras) and consciousness. Simplified, this means clinging to body and mind – i.e. to individual life itself.

Vipassanā: A method of meditation. *One tries to make the mind aware of everything as it arises.*

This is simple. It is not easy. If one can do it, one is face to face with reality itself, the actual continuous flow of one's life. If one perseveres, one comes, by degrees, to understand how everything works; how one's attention is caught by a sense perception, and one is drawn towards it. How this outward reaching leads to actions through thoughts, words and deeds, which have consequences for oneself and others.

It is similar to focusing one's attention, minutely, on the detail of the images which appear on the cinema screen. If one can restrain oneself from being drawn into the story of the film, one comes to see that all these pictures, which succeed each other so rapidly, are none of them real; the fire is not hot, the water is not wet, the heroine is not a real girl. Becoming disenchanted with the illusion of it all, suddenly one sees the screen behind it. Similarly, one has a sudden direct experience of Nibbāna.

Visākha-Pūjā: Visākha is the name of the sixth lunar month. On the full moon of that month, the Buddha was born, became enlightened and passed away into Parinibbāna (died). Pūjā means paying respects. The anniversary of this day every year is celebrated throughout the Buddhist world.

ABOUT THE AUTHOR

Brian F. Taylor was an English poet, philosopher and author. He was born in the spiritual land of India, Darjeeling, where his father served in the British army.

He was educated at St Paul's, Darjeeling, Mercer's School and St Edmund Hall, Oxford where he was Open Scholar in English Language and Literature. He spent two years in the Royal Navy as a Russian linguist.

He taught at the former Royal Pages College in Bangkok where he was head of the Foreign Languages Department. He stayed in a monastery in the northeast of Thailand. He has lectured on Buddhism in New York.

He was a pioneer in Home Education and owned several Antiques Shops in Plymouth, England, specializing in clocks, mechanical music and fireplaces.

He lived a quiet and fulfilling family life around the Noble Eightfold Path in Cornwall and was devoted to the wellbeing and happiness of all Life.

FURTHER READING

BASIC BUDDHISM SERIES
by Brian Taylor

What Is Buddhism?

The Five Buddhist Precepts

Buddhism and Drugs

Basic Buddhist Meditation

The Living Waters of Buddhism

Basic Buddhism for a World in Trouble

Dependent Origination
(An explanation of the Buddha's Paticcasamuppāda)

Samyojana
(The Buddha's Doctrine of the Ten Fetters)

The Five Nivaranas
Buddha's Teaching of the Five Hindrances

Buddhist Pali Chants
(with English translations)

Booklets and kindles are available online from Amazon.

Visit website Universal Octopus
www.universaloctopus.com

www.ingramcontent.com/pod-product-compliance
Lightning Source LLC
Chambersburg PA
CBHW032014040426
42448CB00006B/636